From Believing to Knowing

From Believing to Knowing

Do We Really Know what we Believe?

Carter M. Head

Heads Up Publications

Atlanta

All rights reserved. No part of this book may be reproduced or transmitted in any form or by any means, electronic or mechanical, including photocopying, recording or any information storage and retrieval system without written permission of the author except for brief quotations used in reviews, written specifically for inclusion in a newspaper, blog, magazine, or academic paper.

From Believing to Knowing
Copyright © 2019 by Carter M. Head
Published by Heads Up Publications
Editor: S.L.W.
Cover by Pierre McCummings

ISBN: 978-0-9988323-8-8
Ebook ISBN: 978-0-9988323-9-5
Library of Congress Control Number: 2019943834

Heads Up Publications Books are available at special discounts for bulk purchases for sales or premiums.
Direct all inquiries and correspondence to:
Heads Up Publications
P.O Box 162593
Atlanta, GA 30321
e-mail: headsuppublications@gmail.com

Printed in the United States of America

This Book is dedicated to

The Kingdom of God

Contents

Introduction...................... **IX**

The Authors Disclaimer..................... **XVII**

Chapter 1
We Humans can't Fully Know God..............**23**

Chapter 2
Being Tossed..**29**

Chapter 3
I Don't Believe......................................**41**

Chapter 4
Am I Pushing People Away from God?...........**45**

Chapter 5
Are we Fixing People or Abusing People?........**53**

Chapter 6
A Negative Indictment Against the Faith........**59**

Chapter 7
Liberty in Just Knowing..........................**65**

Chapter 8
Evolving from a Belief System....................**73**

Chapter 9
Perquisites for a Belief System.....................83

Chapter 10
A Quest to Know..89

Chapter 11
Who's Right and Who's Wrong?.......................97

Chapter 12
The Power of Knowing is Contagious............113

Chapter 13
The Conclusion = A Revisiting of What I Know...121

Chapter 14
God or Extraterrestrial the Next Religious Dilemma 135

Chapter 15
For My Christian Pastors and Leadership...143

Introduction

My Motives aren't to try and convert you to join any organization religious or nonreligious. I will be utilizing biblical writing to present some points, I do realize some of you have not and some choose not to subscribe to the Holy Bible, and there are some of you that altogether denounced the Bible's solidity and authenticity. But my use of the Bible is based upon the wide range of usage throughout this world. The Bible is the number one selling book in the world approximately over 3.9 billion and approximately 1 billion given away free. This obviously signifies that the Bible is a valid, interesting, informative and a good source to collaborate gaining a consensus of. I truly respect each of your convictions and beliefs but let's solidify our beliefs, faith systems and ideologies with actually knowing; to really know is proof that we truly have faith in whatever or whoever we believe. There are steps I utilized that helped me come to understand the significance of the severity in advancing in the evolution of my faith in God The Creator and my religious beliefs, especially in my understanding of the Holy Bible of Christianity through research of it. I found that over 100 scriptures warning us about deceptions, temptations, counterfeit influences, consisting of many false prophets and teachers. Here are a few that I observed: 1 Timothy 4:1 now the Spirit expressly says that in later times some will depart from the faith by devoting themselves to deceitful spirits and teaching of demons. Matthew 24:24 for false Christs, and false prophets, will arise and even perform great signs and wonders, deceiving many if possible, even the elect or chosen.

2 Thessalonians 2:9-12 describes a world of lawlessness, pleasure in unrighteousness and strong delusions.

2 Corinthians 4:4 shares that the God of this world has blinded the minds of the unbelievers, to keep them from seeing the light of the gospel of the glory of Christ, who is the image of God.

2 Timothy 3: 1-5 also shares that in the last days there will come times of difficulty, for people will be lovers of self, lovers of money, proud, arrogant, abusive, disobedient to their parents, ungrateful, unholy, heartless,

unappeasable, slanderous, without self-control, brutal, not loving good, treacherous, reckless, swollen with conceit, lovers of pleasure rather than lovers of God, having the appearance of godliness, but denying its powers.

So, this is what prompted me to write this book, because these scriptures and many more tells me that there will be and are many that started out believing and having faith but eventually something happened whereas a great number of people either denounced their faith or just do not believe any more thus confirming the writings in 2 Thessalonians 2:3 that states; for that day will not come until there is a great rebellion against God and a falling away. We must not only be mindful of this possibly happening to us as believers but we must also be vigilant and very knowledgeable of the information that lead us to God and the personal experiences we encounter as a result of knowing and understanding more and more about God The Creator, so that nothing and no one could ever convince, persuade and influence any of us to abolish faith in what we believe. This only will happen when we come to a mindset of knowing, that we know, that we know.

    Understanding that believing and having faith are only prerequisites in our quest to really know without a shadow of a doubt, as it shows us in James 2:19; You believest that there is one God, you doest well: the devils also believe and tremble, but their belief is in vain and our faith will be in vain as well without works. We must work and be persistent in assuring ourselves by knowing that who and what we believe in with faith. Because if we do not, most of us will surely eventually doubt and some willdefinitely fall away from the faith, and maybe even God. Always remember when you have peace within yourself that surpasses all your understanding it will more than likely be because you are in a place or mindset, Knowing God is real in your life.

<u>From Believing to Knowing</u> is my concept of finally knowing God is real, beyond my ability to operate in faith, in order to force myself to believe in a God I really didn't know. I am not saying we should not have faith because mostly everything we do requires us humans to operate in faith, because many things we do on a daily basis we do without any reserve, like sitting in a

chair without worry or doubt because we obviously have faith in the chair not breaking. I am only saying that the organized religious system that many adhere to is the same systems that many are turning from and many are rejecting. I now understand the reasons why…

I believe we all can clearly recognize that a large percentage of believers are leaving churches and their religious affiliations. According to some data research, the number of Americans ages 18-29 who have no religious affiliations has quadrupled in the last 30 years. This book will share with us why and what to do to reverse these exoduses from the church.

It's time to realize belief is a prerequisite to doubt, which is lack of faith, and having unbelief, in which turns into fear and discouragement. This compendium will prompt you to disregard the concept and teaching that are fear based, eventually freeing us up from the mindset of being bound by fear and torment. Does being liberated sound good to you. If it does read this book more than once, enjoy.

The Author's Disclaimer

I acknowledge that the information in the writings of this book is not a disclosure (the act of making new or secret information known). This book is not an attempt to discredit any religious organization nor their beliefs. This book is not an attempt to convert anyone into a certain religious organization. So, I do not accept any responsibility for such suggestions. This book is a testimony of the events in my personal life that extends to my relationship with extends to my relationship with God The Creator as I know God even beyond the Religion concepts. I have chosen to write this book in the wording and exemplifying of God with specific names and pronunciations that are only expressed by the human level of our intellect, according to or learned, earthly dialogue and perceptional constructs.

So in reading, this you will observe me using the name Jesus, Yeshua, Yahweh, God, God The Creator, Most High, Savior, The Christ, and Messiah. Though I do recognize Jesus (Yeshua) as a man, thus utilizing he and him as I refer to Jesus. I do not recognize God as he, nor a she and definite as a it. Here's why… John 1:18 no human has seen God at any time. Exodus 3:20 you can't see my face for there shall no man or human see me and live. Listen no human have ever seen God. Exodus 20:4; you shall not make unto you any graven image or likeness of anything that is in heaven above. Isaiah 55: 8-9 for my thoughts are not your thoughts; neither are your ways my ways. For as the heavens are higher than the earth, so are my ways higher than your ways, and my thoughts than your thoughts. Numbers 23:19 God is not a man, so he does not lie; God is not a human, so God does not change God's mind. Job 26:26 behold (observe regard) God is great and we do not (understand) God. Romans 11:33 oh, the depth of the riches both of the wisdom and knowledge of God! How unsearchable are His judgments and His ways past finding out! But Paul made this statement and I do likewise in Philippians 3:8 I count all things but loss for the excellency of the knowledge of Christ Jesus my Lord! That I may know Him, and the power of His Resurrection not as though I had already attained, either were I already perfect or fully mature, but I choose to follow after so that I may apprehend and this one thing I do, forgetting those things which are behind, and reaching forth unto those things which are before, I press toward the mark for the price of the high calling of God in Christ Jesus. Let us all, therefore as many as be fully mature be thus minded.

No one human knows it all in reference to God. But we all should be more seriously sincere about achieving information and having personal experiences that will confirm and solidify the little we have obtained actually to know of God. At least on our personal level, enough that no one can't ever influence us not to believe, have faith in and know about God.

My target audience is the people that are contemplating and considering, throwing away their bibles, leaving the church, and maybe denouncing God, the people that have already left church and Religion (because of being persuaded and influenced) and the people that never believed in God. This is not a book that's preaching a saving message. I can't save anyone, God saves.

1

We Humans can't Fully Know God...

John 1:18 declares; no human has seen God at any time. Only the Christ. So, the only true knowledge of God proceeds only from the Messiah. Christ revealed God the Creator unto us humans by love because God was hidden under the shadows of the law, so our minds were not able to perceive God but by the Savior. In Isaiah 55:9; God declares to the prophet Isaiah that as far as the heavens are higher than the earth, so are God's ways higher than our ways and Gods thoughts than our thoughts.

In Exodus 33:20 God declared that no human could see God's face and live, but in Exodus 33 later in the chapter, God tells Moses, "I will cause my goodness to pass in front of you and I will proclaim my name, the Lord, in your presence. So, when I express that I now know God, I mean; In the goodness and essence of Love by way of the Messiah who expressed Gods love, mercy, power wisdom, compassion, peace, grace, forgiveness, healing, and comfort through his character. Even though, humans of that time were still limited to what they knew about God and the Christ. John 21:25 shares; there are also many other things which Christ did, in which, if they should be written, the world itself could not contain the books that should be written. Be careful when people try to convince you that they hear, see or know so much about God. Even the disciples that walked with Christ only knew a small portion of who God really is.

Just know we as humans, no matter how many degrees, titles, schooling and encounters we have, we all are still limited in our knowledge of God, it does not matter how much we fast, pray, preach, speak in tongue, tarry at altars, and proclaim we have the Holy

Spirit, we all are still limited in our knowledge, thoughts and understanding of who God ultimately is. Because the capacity of our human minds and brains is finite, having limits or bound, even if our brains ever operate at 100 percent full capacity. Why... Because God is an infinite God and God's thoughts will always and forever be far passed our thoughts and total understanding.

    Let's not allow any human to put God in the box of their particular religious beliefs. We must understand that the Creator God is limitless or endless in space, extent or size, impossible to be measured or calculated. God's infinity is in God's love, goodness and mercy, which are all limitless and unmeasurable without end. God is omniscient, all knowing, all wise and all-seeing, God is omnipresent, universal, all present, infinite, everywhere at the same time. Even beyond the concept of time and space even beyond earthly laws of physics. God is divine angelic, seraphic, excellent and greatly. God is sovereign, a supreme ruler, absolute, unrestricted, ultimately, unrestrained and boundless. God is omnipotent having unlimited power, almighty, preeminent and the most high.

There's no way, any human would really know the gender of God, though many of us, use the male gender description. All these descriptions and characteristics are expressed by words and terms derived from mere mortals or finite human capabilities. So, we can only recognize God the Creator by and through The Christ exemplifying and representing the true essence of God the Creator in a way we humans could and can comprehend. Christ as a witness and example in human form that God is real. We humans, also by our personal experiences with the true essence, the intrinsic nature or indispensable quality of God were taught characteristics and goodness, though mainly abstract measures existing in thought, that's confirmed within our own souls, spirit, heart and nature, especially by unconditional love, forgiveness, mercy and grace.

So yes, I truly know God the Creator as described love, mercy, power and forgiveness on a personal level towards me and within me with assurance and truth, so I hold dear to what I know myself.

2

Being Tossed

What I am referring to when I used this word tossed; is that many people fluctuate on a consistent basis depending on whatever their emotional feelings lead them at any such time.

They are conformed by moving from place to place, from ideology to ideology, from doubting to believing and to moving on from being stagnant or dormant. Being tossed can be detrimental to a person of faith and belief system. Ephesians 4:14 shares why: "That we henceforth be no more children, tossed to and fro, carried about with every wind of doctrine or teachings by the trickery of humans and cunning cleaveness, whereby they lie in wait to deceive." This happens because many believers walk in vanity or futility of their mind and having the understanding darkened, being alienated from the life of God through ignorance in them, because of the blindness of their heart, through past feelings, given themselves over unto lasciviousness to work all uncleaness with greediness and lust.

So, we all must be renewed in the Spirit of our minds by increasing in the knowledge of God the creator. We must continually advance in our relationship with God, by informing ourselves with more knowledge of the essences of Gods love and being. Most faith-filled believers have been taught that God is in control of our every operation on a daily basis thus causing them to have a mindset of slothfulness with very little effort towards solidifying what they know in God. Be reminded faith without works is dead.

Many will sit back and wait on God to figure everything out for them and make things happen for them without themselves doing anything but praying, believing and receiving. We must understand God put us humans in charge of our efforts, allowing us humans to do or don't do; God gave us all the mandate of choice. What happens for us is mainly up to us as individuals, not God. Yes, God is all knowing and yes, we are predestinated according to God's will. But God foreknow whether or not we would do or not do. God foreknow whether or not we would obtain more information in an effort to really know in order for our believing with faith in God would occur consistency, never doubting. Please, never believe the hype when people speak as declaring they and we can control and command and also by God's blessing.

So, the knowing is for us to maintain our walk with God with consistency and assurance without ever doubting or turning because we have lack of faith due to even severe consequences. Unbelief will never be in our mindsets once we choose to operate in knowing. Too many of our belief systems are being shaken by the trails, test, confusions of life. Living in a world of technology we all are privy to an abundance of information at our leisure and most of the information we see, hear and experience is only propaganda and lies. Thus, causing many to turn from and be tossed to and fro by that power of persuasion and the power of suggestion.

Please do not be deceived. God does exist around us, within us, beyond us and before us everywhere. God is definitely bigger than any belief system. God is greater than any book. God is wiser than all Religion and their teachings and their ideologies. This is why we all must know God for ourselves. When you and I come to that mindset and place of peace within ourselves that surpasses all of our understandings are we then more than likely to have finally obtained a fact of knowing that God is real in our life, standing on that fact no matter what we see hear, think or experience. We must stand assured in what we know without being tossed or lead astray with the ideologies, teachings, lies, lack, propaganda and negative experiences that usually conditions and persuades us to move from what we believe, have faith in and know.

Beware, people are so charismatic and persuasive they've convinced many to believe in what they promulgate, information that is untrue and fabulous, sometimes unknowingly. Lots of teachers, instructors, ministers, and leaders are misinformed with false history and they tend to repeat the false teachings of that fake history. The confusion comes when they teach the false information; then we receive the information, then we accept the information as fact, afterword's, some of us with inquiring minds go forward in obtaining more information from other sources we usually either find out the error of the previous teachings or we are swayed and influenced to receive and follow another lie thus causing more confusion. This is why we must be rooted and grounded on what we know, in our hearts.

Allow me to give you an example of people using false history and then sharing a truth about the false history, but then using that truth in order to influence and persuade those that once believed the false history, to now believe and follow everything they say and do. Here we go again being tossed to and fro. Here is a perfect example of what I am referring to. For centuries, in movies, books, certain bible illustration, television, cartoons, pictures placed in churches, homes and public institutions depicts God, Jesus and Angels, and Bible characters as being European people. Many of us were persuaded to believe, follow and promote that white imagery to our children and grandchildren. But once we researched history, we found out that we have been taught a bunch of lies in reference to Biblical understandings of the race and ethnicity of the people in scripture and the false narratives associated with those characters.

Even in slavery times in American History, those of us that research has found out about how slave owners controlled slaves with what is called the Slave Bible; which deleted many chapters of the Bible only implementing the scriptures on obeying masters. But after obtaining more truth about our history in Biblical time, some of us tend to now reject the whole Bible and questions its authenticity after believing in it all our lives. Some even move away from the church, the Bible and their belief in the God of the Bible. We must be mindful and careful not to denounce what we know to be true to us as individuals. We must hold dear to that which has given us hope and peace within our minds and hearts in reference to our real relationships with God.

    Yes, we have been taught in some cases, things that are erroneous to scripture and God the Creator. But those false teachings should not have the power and confusion to move us from what we have experienced, felt and understood in conjunction with how God loves us on a personal level. It is our own testimony. Hold dear to your testimony, research history and be able to do it with reasoning and mainly confirmation of facts. Just know in the case as I have just shown, just because God and Jesus are not European, does not mean or suggest they are not real in your heart, mind, soul, and spirit.

Please do not allow anyone, any negative situation, any feeling, any thought nor any new information, detour you from or cause you to reject or denounce your belief and your faith in what you once believed, by just knowing that you know that you, know from your own personal intuition and assurance. Do not ever allow it to happen to you. Avoid this by being careful and mindful that all rhetoric and new revelations are coming from another flawed finite human that's only operating with approximately 10 to

15 percent cannot of their brain capacity to know. Just allow what they believe as truth, to be their truth for them. But hold on to your truth in God, it's more important for you than their truth is for you and your transformation.

3

I Don't Believe

Invalid beliefs mean that we have to accept and adhere to something as truth because another person shared information to us to convince us of a thing, system or concept. They also ask us to continue to have confidence in what they shared with us and propagate that if we do not believe, we are then justly condemned with valid and good reason. So, I say believing is a flawed construct designed to control people with the use of administrating false hope to it replicates. Because whatever you have to convince me to believe will always be subject to disbelief even after sometimes years of believing. Belief systems, set people up for doubt, unbelief and then fear.

Be reminded when we operate in knowing we do not need to believe because we now know and to know does not require a belief system. A person will never doubt what they know. It is time to transcend and go beyond pass beliefs systems that requires faith with no rational. <u>Faith without thought is false</u>

<u>hope, because true faith is complete trust or confidence in.</u> But we all can agree that no matter how long we have been conditioned to believe and have faith in something, there have been and will always be times when we come to a place and mindset of not believing and not having been totally confident in a thing. When this occurs, the religious sect calls it: little or lack of faith and that statement moves a person towards even more unbelief and discouragement. This is the danger of walking in belief versus knowing mentality and spirituality after being taught to have faith and just to believe I came to an understanding, freedom, and enthusiasm as some people did in the bible who once believed because of what another person said and taught into the mindset of acknowledging their point of finally knowing. John chapter 4

is a biblical passage of scripture that shares this declaration of moving from believing to knowing so profoundly it was liberating for me, and I hope for you as well. As verses 39 through 42, when the men believe what she said but after they saw Jesus themselves, all of them said; Now, we know He is the Christ.

You have to agree; we all knew first, then we forgot, then we retaught error, then some of us reconsidered, by thinking, reflecting and realizing and then came evolution and growth which entails, acquired knowledge that overrides, indoctrination and influence and through it all, some us have come to know… Oh, it is so liberating and peaceful.

4

Am I Pushing People Away from God?

Wouldn't it be sad and concerning if you one day realized you were an intricate part in the "falling away from the church" (people leaving religion and God all together)? I am sure you would be saddened by your efforts even unknowingly and unintentionally, causing people to be offended by what you've said to the point of them operating in apostasy, which is an abandonment or renunciation of religious or political belief. Well, it should bother you because it surely dismayed me, as being a Preacher of the Gospel of Jesus The Christ and the Kingdom of God; I started my ministry by and with strong and hard rebuke, correcting and chastisements and used biblical scripture to propagate it. I really spoke with meanness and harshness in my delivery of the biblical teachings. I now know I used that method in order to scare people into conforming to change in their lives. I never meant for this method of hellfire preaching to be done because I was angry with people. I did it because I actually loved people and desired them all to be changed from doing sinful acts, so my motives were correct and with good measure. But I come to find out through reconnecting with some of the people I preached to, that it hurt them mentally and caused them to leave the church. Though some I've talked to understood my hard preaching and critical teaching was for their good. But I have always wondered; how many never went back to any church, how many are now caught up in new age religious ideologies and how many are being led astray by voices on social media and the internet. Just know, I often ask God to forgive me and I pray those that were hurt by my preaching would forgive me as well. Some of you ministers reading this probably think this method of preaching is good and it's just what the nonbelievers need. But please ask yourself; why would anyone honestly love a God that would kill their children, cause them to have accidents, cause them to lose money for not tithing, bring confusion amongst their marriages, bring sickness and curses upon them and their love ones and then send them to a devils hell full of fire because they sin and make mistakes, but you say after all this; God loves you.

I am writing this for all of us to humble ourselves and reconsider our ways, realizing we are all flawed as human beings. In the book of Jeremiah 31:3, God clearly states: I've loved them with everlasting love, therefore with loving-kindness have I drawn them. Yes, we can pull up scripture all through the Bible in reference to correcting people, even punishing people, I call this proof-texting. We all better pray and hope this fire and brimstone; fear-based theology is not the heart of God for God's people's demise. Because if it is, we all are doomed for fire in hell.

Listen; I am not saying not to correct, I am only saying: If any of us are prompt to rebuke, correct and chastise anyone, whether in a church or religious setting and maybe even within our own family and friends or associations with others, we must only do minister in and with love, along with much empathy and compassion as possible. First Timothy 5:1 teaches us to rebuke not an elder but intreat or appeal to them as they were your parents, with honor and respect. Let's examine how Jesus did it. In the book of John chapter 8 and verse 7; Jesus said unto all those who declared rebuke, chastisement, and death upon a sinful woman, "You without sin, go ahead and throw the first rock and stone her to death for her sin." Not one of them was able to stone her because all humans sin. But the way Jesus handled her sin was with empathy and compassion of her flawed nature as a mere human and told her "woman no one condemned you and neither do I so go and do not do that sin anymore."

Jesus said in Matthew 5:17-20, "Think not that I am come to destroy the law or the prophets, but I come to fulfill it." Jesus came to fulfill the law in and by loving us so much he gave his life as a ransom for us to be redeemed from the curse of the law (Galatians 3:13). Jesus preached and taught law but only with and by grace.

Today, we must only teach law, with grace and love governing our motives and hearts. Because if you continue to preach law, hell and fire, condemning and judgmental messages without a heart of grace, being empathetic to the cause, having much compassion, and you hurt more people, you will definitely be a part of the cause in many running away from the Gospel, the church and some denouncing God.

Remember Jesus stated in Matthew 5:20; "For I say unto you, that except your righteousness exceed the righteousness of the scribes and Pharisees you shall in no case enter into the Kingdom of Heaven." So, I guess you will not get into heaven and you will most surely try to prevent others from entering as well. Jesus describes this in Mathew 23:13: "Woe unto you, scribes and Pharisees, hypocrites, for you shut up the kingdom of heaven against people, for you neither go in yourselves, neither allow you them that are entering to go in."

Please don't be a blocker. Please do not be a hindrance nor a stumbling block. Move! In order for others to see the real Christ in the church. Most of us are in the way of the true essence of Christ and His love. Please stop running people away from God with your words, your character, your lack of knowledge, your greed and your fantasy of fame, prestige, and power.

I declare I'm no longer operating in what we call spiritual abuse. Thank God! For my change of heart in this area. I never desire to be part of the problem. Do you?

5

Are we fixing people or Abusing People?

Religion is not a bad word in all instances. In James Chapter 1:27 the Bible speaks of pure and undefiled religion before our God, is to visit the fatherless and widows in their affliction and to keep yourself from being polluted or corrupted of this world. To be religious is to be saintly, prayerful, churchgoing, committed, and practicing in the belief system you choose. I hear a lot of church goers declaring they are not religious, but they go to church every week and are consistently operating their doctrinal belief system and have been for years. I think some denounced the word religion because they've seen many religious sects hurt lots of people all over the world. I would assume there is a negative indictment against religious groups in the eyes and mind of the religious people. "Go, figure."

    Listen it's ok to be religious in your views, ideologies, and theology, only when your views are helping all humans and not hurting some humans. Remember, church and religion are supposed to be spiritual safe places and sound truth of enlightenment in reference to God The Creator, for all people. But there are so many religious groups that have leaders using their spiritual authority and titles to control, manipulate and have dominance over others, in order to meet their financial needs, sexual desires and spiritual superiority. Some leaders use shame, fear, and judgmental condemnation or guilt through legalism by sharing God's so call disapproval of a person. This is what some us call, spiritual abuse and the results are drastically alarming. Because of spiritual abuse, many people are being hurt and many more are being convinced just to leave the church altogether. So, I ask are we hurting or helping the people? When I refer to the "hurting people" I mean people that are in need of help, solace, knowledge, and love, people who are in some cases less fortunate, abused, trapped, confused, unhealthy and mislead. They come to church attempting to develop a relationship with religion and God. But end up being misled again and abused again.

How does spiritual abuse occur in the life of a hurting person? The religious or spiritual abuse happens as a result of some leaders promoting and demanding people to live up to a spiritual standard and performances that are extra hard to live up to at all times for the rest of our lives. The leaders are not even living up to all the standards they are attempting to get others to abide by, leaving some of the hurting to be enslaved into lawful and doctrinal bondages, thus causing the already hurting people to have the desire to be free! Free from what you may ask? Liberalized from whatever religious bondage you've put them under.

So, in your effort to help are you unknowingly pushing people away from The Real and True Living Creator God that's in the Essence of The Christ? Be reminded, The Christ-like life begins with liberty and salivation from dead, sinful works that once governed a person's life. And if you are a person that's been hurt by religion and religious people, you must understand that God needs you free because God loves us all, unconditionally. God gave us a savior in Christ Jesus in order to accomplish that. It is your responsibility to learn of Him, seek God and fall in love with God after you get to know God as being real in your life. Then and only then will you be able to sustain your growth in God and once you really know God is real, I believe each of us will at that point become better, loving and caring people, that no one could ever convince, that God is not real. We have to know God pass all people and their negative influences.

6

A Negative Indictment Against the Faith

Most Religious beliefs explain the reasons it views, and teachings are valid in reference to propagating the concept of fear-based theology it's due to the interpretation of biblical writings and according to their understanding, humans are to revere God, revere means to feel deep respect or admiration for and to hold in high esteem. I concur, but where I disagree is the use of the word reverence causing as convincing a person, to accept, admire, respect, hold in high regard and love with your whole heart because of you being convinced to be afraid and frightened of the terrible fate, this God will administer to a person that does not believe according to their specific teachings. Is not this totally fear based (a person prompting another to be scared of the same God because that God will harm you, condemn you, kill you and send Gods creation to a place of fire) and if some of us accept and adhere to this concept are we doing it because we are afraid not to. That is not true honor of God, that is not accepting the true love of God in our hearts, so most pretend to honor, respect and love that God; because it is impossible to really love a God that supposed to love us unconditionally. But at the same time seems to abhor us because of our decisions God created us a human to be flawed and operate in because of our fleshly tendencies.

    I find it difficult to really and truly love a God that torments the very creation put in place to be loved. Love and fear are not and should not ever be put in collaboration with one another; it's an oxymoron; it contradicts its self in any rationalized concept in reference to a God of Love. Why have humans accepted the concept of being afraid of God and having honor and admiration for God at the same time? This requires a special and unique type of faith, and this type of faith causes doubt, unbelief and denouncing the type of God, that they are taught to fear, not reference.

Be reminded faith shouldn't be blind and full of ignorance; faith should not mean disregarding reality, truth, sound, rational and intellectual thinking and consideration by human reasoning. Because thinking, reasoning, research, and intellect is a prerequisite to knowing. I desire like many of us, to know, not just believe because all beliefs are subject to change with the next intellectual and charismatic teacher. We need to operate in knowing.

Christianity or any other Religion does not have to be with ignorance; people that accept religion do not have to be naive or gullible. We should always be consciously awake. Allowed or even encouraged to think and reason within ourselves as well as listen and learn from others. Why should we be forced to believe everything another human believes. The very thing they are attempting to convince us to believe they probably will eventually doubt themselves; they call themselves Ex-Pastors. Beliefs often change and evolve into a better and more sufficient way of thinking. This is why coming into knowledge should be our quest to know without any doubting.

7

Liberty in Just Knowing

All of us humans are being influenced at areas of our lives from birth into adulthood whether it be through and by subliminal, Religion, traditions, government, culture, environment, surroundings, family, televisions, internet, and even our own self-realizations and intellect. At some point, these avenues of mental exploits and indoctrinated influences that most of us have or will adhere to are mainly the force behind systematic imagery that solidifies who we are and what we tend to believe at least until we are liberated. We must understand that most of the ideologies we are taught are mere propaganda designed to keep us bound and constrained to the point of submission to particular man-made constructs, that conditions a portion of us humans who do not have the knowledge, means, courage, and enthusiasm to advance into a more glorified people designed and created by God for God glory to be expressed in and by love on earth with peace towards all humanity. But this concept of holding us humans down is falling apart because of the consistency in the mindset of many people to be at peace within and eagerness to do and be more in the world for humanity sake as a whole full of prosperity beyond a select few, but the betterment of all humans.

This eagerness is driving many of us to reevaluate, reconsider, rethink and revise the whole concept of life and having life more abundantly. It is opening us up to be free to think, research, asks questions, seek answers and become consciously aware with peace in doing so, without fear of opposition and condemnation from other people who do not see as we are beginning to see. Some call it a woke generation; I call it liberty to who God created me to be and to return to that person that God originally designed me to be.

So, when I came upon a scripture in the Bible in Ecclesiastes Chapter 3 verses 9 through verse 15 where it shares that God made everything beautiful in its time and that God has set the world in our heart so that no human can find out the work that God made from the beginning to the end. That humans should understand that there is negativity in humans, but we are to rejoice still and do good in our individual lives. That we humans should enjoy the good of our laboring for it is a gift of God. Because what God does it shall be forever, and nothing can be put to it nor anything taken from it. God declares "That which hath been is now; and that which is to be hath already been; and God requireth that which is past." This confirms to me that; though influences, propaganda, MK Ultra, science relation, conditioning, subliminal and even fear. No one and nothing can stop us from being who God originally designed us to be unless we allow and permit it to overtake us to the point of we not waking up consciously and beginning to reason within ourselves with intellect sound and research that accomplished with peace of mind.

So, I now choose to operate in love and peace knowing God is real no matter what influences come my way. My mind is made up; knowing not just believing but knowing Creator God is real and is unconditional love. Ask me how I know; it is because I experienced the love of God on a personal level, due to an encounter on this Earth that interrupted consumed and embellished me to the point of me physically seeing love, thinking love, realizing love and operating in love. Knowing God love me so much that I could experience this encounter with love opposite of the religion I had previously been influenced by. So, after this amazing episode, I came upon confirmation as I read John Chapter 4 in the King James Bible how those people first believed and then transitioned to eventually knowing. Along with that passage of scripture from Ecclesiastes Chapter 3 that also enlightened me to the fact that I once knew, then I forgot, then I was influenced that I reconsider that I knew again and now I am free, and as of now I am at liberty because I know God is real and God loves me unconditionally. Job declared in chapter 19, verse 25: For I know that my Redeemer liveth. I, somewhat like Jeremiah in Lamentations chapter 3 verses 21 – 2, I recall to my mind, therefore, I have hope. You and I have to continually remind ourselves of Gods greatness and love towards us no matter what comes upon us to convince us that God is not for us.

8

Evolving from a Belief System

Our beliefs construct should be progressive, some faster than others, some Religions and Spiritualist calls it enlightenment or being woke. Be reminded most all of us have slightly different interpretations and perceptions of the biblical writings. So, we must ask… who's actually right, what religious truth should we choose to believe and follow being there are thousands of religious views, organizations, beliefs, and denominations.

    Should any of us wholeheartedly trust and believe another humans heart, mind, and understanding unto the point of never questioning, doubting, or even remotely discrediting their point throughout the rest of our lives, disregarding any new information, discoveries, personal experiences and evolved understandings. Maybe most of us will not ever discredit nor oppose the human or humans that we have believed in their writings and teachings for many years of our lives at the cost of we being uncomfortable, confused or bewildered to the point of operating in doubt in those beliefs and concepts taught to us.

    Most of us then live our lives struggling with questionable truths secretly, due to the fear of being called a heretic, a devil, a lost soul and a person that has been tricked to backslide or turn from a set belief system. So, we continue to pretend we believe and through the motions like the Nicolaitans did in Revelation the second chapter and verses 14 through 15. These people were considered to be make-believe Christians. I do not think any of us Christians would approve of being called fake, so many just keep it a secret that they have doubts and see the contradictions in the Bible. Remember we have been taught from Biblical scripture that doubting and lack of belief is a big sin.

    I wrote a book called Lying Mirrors and, in that book, my main objective was to help the reader to consider their ways and look into their hearts and determine whether or not they were actually true to themselves without fear of oppositions and rejections. Could the mere fact that most of us in religion are afraid to progress, evolve and understand according to our hearts and perceptions because we do not desire to be rejected, ostracized or belittled. Due to us openly expressing our personal views in reference to religion and the traditions we were raised on that are obliviously flawed and do not seem to be benefitting humanity at all. Realizing this, should not we be more enthused about moving from whatever the religious constructs we have held dear to, unto a mindset of really knowing. We should choose not to be depressed, confused and uncomfortable with teaching from others that is just not working for us as individuals. Should not we have a right to move toward a peace that comes with knowing without all the doctrines and belief systems that comes with religion?

Say these words with me; I am moving on from believing towards knowing with assurance that one day I will know that I know that I know. So again, for you not to be confused in this chapter, believing and having faith in what we have read and been taught by other humans is a definite prerequisite towards eventually knowing. Having a belief in the Bible and what it teaches can most definitely help and assist us all in our quest to actually operate according to what we absolutely know now to be the Truth... But we must not continue in the concept of only believing because we all realize no matter how much faith and belief, we have some time the cares of this worlds and negative experiences cause us to doubt. To fall short of the faith walk we have been taught to walk and operate in, prompting a lot of us religious folk to turn, not only from religion but also eventually turning from God or believing in whether or not there is a God at all. This book hopefully will prevent this from happening to you because I know now that God is real in the essence and embodiment of love and I do not need anybody's faith or belief system to accept that as my fact and my truth.

    I having faith in God, believing in Christianity and believing in the Bible, but doubting, researching secretly caused me to come close to not only losing my religion and moving from a church setting it almost caused me to move toward denouncing God. God Is real, and I will never again trust in a religious system and doctrine to validate or fulfill my understanding with beliefs that can and will be tested. I choose to know, which never can be tried, tested, disproved and never set me up for doubt.

 Again, we have to start out by believing and having faith, but that is for babes, it is milk, and scriptures instruct us to move off of milk and desire the sincere meat of the word. It is called moving on into maturity. This is where we will experience more evidence of God sovereignty, love, forgiveness, mercy, grace, and power. Because God is love and God is real, and God is good.

Experiencing evidence proves we do not have to believe nor have faith in what we have already experienced. We then know and there is no need to convince yourself that you should utilize faith in what you know in order to sustain or convince you of the evidence that actually solidified what you now know. Many religious leaders teach; faith is believing in unverified information, but more knowledge adds questions to our faith and life's facts promote doubts, resulting in loss of hope. We should not continue in the type of faith that requires believing. We all need to adhere to the type of faith that prompts and encourages us to come to the point of knowing.

Just know it's ok to think for yourself, its ok to research, it is ok to ask questions, it is ok to revise and reconsider your beliefs. It's an excellent place to start your quest towards knowing when you are uncomfortable and confused with what you have been taught. It is ok to come to know ourselves and who or what lives within us. We must understand your truth may not be my truth and that's ok. Its ok to respect other people views but they also have to respect our views and make peace with all people for the sake of having peace. Knowledge is power!!

9

Prerequisites for a Belief System

How do we begin the process of not only believing but knowing? We must first acknowledge that signs and wonders are a form of evidence that we see. Jesus told Thomas to "Except you see my hands and feel the hole in my side, you won't believe." Jesus also revealed to doubting Thomas; Blessed are they that have not seen and yet have believed.

Our beliefs should not always have to be solidified by touch, sight, feelings, signs, and miracles. If our belief system is predicated by evidence, this only means physical or carnal experiences are prerequisites for a belief system, in which most religions teach and propagate. We must come to understand, lack of physical experiences causes doubt in every case where people are holding on the concept of believing. Their beliefs turn into doubt when there is no obvious and convincing evidence by signs and wonders occurring their situations.

Most people pray, beg and believe with their whole heart for God to do as they need, and most must admit at times, need they prayed for, never manifested. Causing, not only doubt or disbelief but also causes frustrations, anger, unbelief, depression and even a turning away from God the Creator and the Messiah, solely based on signs and wonders or whether or not our prayers are answered in the manner we desire. We must be mindful, not to solidify our relationship with God the Creator and the Messiah, only based on signs and wonders or whether or not our prayers are answered in the manner we desire. Because so many are not only leaving the church, but many are also moving from even acknowledging God as real. These are people that have believed and been involved in some type of religious belief most of their lives.

    This is why it's of most urgency that we all move on forward towards actually coming to a mindset of knowing without of ever doubting or being convinced by influence from: social media, news propaganda, YouTube, informers, testimonies of ex-pastors and ex Christians, books that suggest God is not real, explanations from scientists, listening to atheist, looking at the hypocrisy in religion and lack of love, empathy and compassion for all humans. Because all of these and more, are entities that will prompt and cause those of us that only operate in a belief construct, to doubt and turn from that belief or beliefs eventually. Unless we all hold dear to that which we now know, my grandmother once said, and I quote "I know that I know that I know" unquote, now that is the kind of knowing I desired to have from the being of my interest in God and the Bible. I have always just wanted the whole truth and nothing but the truth. But throughout my walk-in life I have come to understand that there are many expressed truths from the individual mindset and level of knowledge received from different sources of influence that connect to different people in different places and in different times. In an individual's circle, some information's received and believed as truth, for some will not be believed truth by others.

Most information that is considered truth to many is not truth to all. So, the motive of me writing this compendium is not directed to solidify my truth versus your truth. It is to bring an awareness of the reasons for confusions, disarray and discouragements that comes with the construct of only believing. Believing is not fail-proof; it is flawed on so many levels of understanding. This book is to encourage and prompt many of us believers to be consistent and persistent in a valid effort to begin a quest in not only believing but also knowing. I now suggest that knowing and believing always brings forth a peace that surpasses our human experiences, our human understandings, and our religious views and worldly ideologies.

    The question has been asked: How do I and where do I start in my quest to know without doubting? I will answer this and many more questions in the next chapter. Please continue reading.

10

A Quest to Know

There are two types of knowing, the knowing that is most common in the world of religion that is taught in most churches is to be aware of through observation, inquiry or information. This type of knowing requires being animated sometimes dramatic in teaching and preaching. This type of knowing also requires outward appearances of grandeur. This concept of knowing is solidified by evidence of the manifestations of healings, deliverances, promotions, prophecies and increase monetarily. But when the evidence fails to occur this type of knowing dissipate and causes many believers to begin to doubt again.

    The type of knowing that my heart desires you to operate in is to develop and have a relationship with God the Creator through meeting and spending time with God and becoming familiar with God essence. God's essence is Agape love without ever doubting that type of love and not ever opening your mind up to be convinced or influenced that the God of Creation is not real in your life. It is a choice and a decision that can only be made by us as individuals, in conjunction with studying theology encountering God's presence by the essence of God's being. Also listening to the testimonies of the witnesses of the Messiah, The Christ, The God of Salvation whom I believe to be Yeshua (one proposed transliteration of the Hebrew or Aramaic name of Jesus commonly used by individuals in the sacred name movements). Though there will be times, we all will experience signs and wonders (evidence). Be mindful that when there is no evidence, we will still know God is real because we now have heard God within our cluttered minds and hearts.

I now know we humans are designed with a conscience and the humans consist of a concept of knowing right and wrong before we are taught it. There is a scripture in the Bile there share these words: " For when the Gentile which have not the law, do by nature the things contained in the law, these, having not the law, are a law unto themselves: which show the work of the law written in their hearts, their conscience also bearing witness." Romans chapter 2 verses 14 and 15. Just come to know confirmation is administered within our hearts. God sees and deals with the hearts of humans.

    The truth and realness of God's existence in my life and me not doubting, actually solidifies me knowing God is real without a taught belief system that is flawed and based on worldly experiences. This worldly construct, we exist in, consist of influences, ideologies, laws, lies, misunderstandings, false doctrines, bad teachers, religious beliefs, hatred, lack of love and so many other things to discourage us as human beings thus causes many of us believers of God to consider denouncing God existences. Be careful and be mindful, but most of all be consistent and persistent in being open to listen from within. Beware of what your conscience is saying, study, research and confirm information especially theology, follow your good moral values, never be in bondage to no other human or leader. Do not be boxed not any religion or cult, be open-minded. Be ok with thinking for yourself at times, allow love, forgiveness, and compassion to flow through your mind towards all humans.

Be free and at liberty with expressing your understanding of your truths, have a cordial, constructive dialogue with others understanding we all will disagree in love, not with hatred. Do good towards all people. Be ok with who you really are, loving who God created you to be in this world. Having peace within even when some reject you, be open for correction. Be comfortable reconsidering your own ways by being honest with yourself. Rethink some things you and I were taught in error or misinterpretations.

    Redo your system of believing especially when it causes you to doubt and do not be afraid to sometimes follow your intuition, your gut feelings and your Godly wisdom. I know you will find a greater level of knowledge about you and God that will solidify and confirm God the Creator is real in your life and you won't ever doubt that again. Thank you for being serious about moving forward in your quest to know God and go from not only believing but eventually knowing that you know that you know.

11

Who's Right and Who's Wrong?

In this chapter we will discover one of Religions biggest dilemma's and that is; the big confusion, frustration and fighting about which Religion is telling the whole truth and nothing but the truth... Now, if you do not think of this as a dilemma in your life, it is probably because you have suggested and have believed most of your life, being convinced that your belief system and what you come to understand is the truth. As a result, having been solidified by your agreement of that credence (your belief in or acceptance of something as true). But what makes for the dilemma, is when you become open to listen to, converse with by reasoning together with others of a different credence but with reserve, realizing that maybe probable cause to examine through extensive research the legitimacy of their claim, and afterwards discovering that there may be some solidarity to them and some relatable consensus. Even in disagreeing with what that person is sharing makes for a dilemma being formed within your mindset in which you ponder on continually. Also being able to rethink or reconsider some things you have been taught in your religious ideology from church, family, culture, and associations with your belief system. This is now a dilemma! When the difficult choice has to be made between two or more alternatives or beliefs, it can cause confusions, frustrations, opposition and the denouncing of one or more beliefs we were so once adamant in our stance about. But now since we have been convinced otherwise some of us tend to publicly declare, criticize, discredit and condemn what we once stood up for.

    We must contend with the questions of; why do we believe one is right, and the others are wrong… Why are we eventually becoming convinced that someone else of another belief system is right and we obviously were wrong all the while...? Well maybe because of the power of persuasion and the power of suggestion which are the sometimes-taught ability to convince others. Obviously, you reading this compendium have to mean you, and I are dealing with this dilemma, know someone who is and maybe have dealt with this in their lives at some point in the past. In either case, I believe this book will help alleviate the traits of the dilemma of answering the questions; who is right and who is wrong?

      My motives in writing this book is also to prompt us to get to a place of really advancing in what we know and moving to a mindset of peace by not needing proof that God The Creator is real. Let's talk about the Bible. Why not, being that the Bible is the number one selling book in the world and the most read in the world, approximately 3.9 billion copies sold over the last 50 years. So, this means even when it is the most misunderstood, misinterpreted and misused books, it still has relevance even if you do not believe in its solidity and truths. So, I am going to quote something from it to make my points clear on why there is such a big dilemma within our mindsets in reference to religion and our beliefs. 1Timothy Chapter 4 warns us that there will be times that some of us believers would depart from the faith, giving heed to seducing doctrines of the destroyers. Matthew the 24th chapter shares to us Believers that there will be many false teachers or prophets that will deceive many by showing great signs and wonders, as did Simon the Sorcerer in Acts 8 who used magic to bewitch or confuse the people of Samaria giving out that he himself was some great one. The Samaritans even said, he was of the great power of God, yes even the leaders in Samaria. But when Philip the evangelist went down to the city of Samaria and preached Christ unto them, they all believed, especially when Philip preached the things concerning the Kingdom of God and theme of Jesus the Christ. Simon himself also believed and was baptized.

Now, I realized that some of you that are considering leaving your belief in Jesus because through research you found that the Christ and The Savior could not have been called Jesus because the J was invented in the 1600s, I suggest you research why. For the sake of alleviating any arguments and causing anyone not to get the premise of this book, I will say the Hebrew form of the name: Yeshua. I do not think we have to be stuck on the spelling of the name as long as you know that he was The Christ, The Messiah and Christ is not Yeshua or Jesus last name. I have to believe in by faith as the Savior of the world. Let's not reduce our faith and denounce The Christ with a play on letters. This is another reason why you should move on to knowing, in order not to be persuaded to leave Christ because of the spellings of his name. It is time to be of the mindset of not being deceived so easily as instructed in 2nd Thessalonians 2nd chapter and Revelation Chapter 16. Be careful that you are not following people because of signs and wonders.

    The number one cause for an alarming rate of believers leaving the church,

Christianity, their religious beliefs, and eventually denouncing God is because of other people (humans). Though some believers tend to contribute their departure from fellowship with other believers as so-called church hurt. Church hurt means to some the organizations as a whole has damaged a person, mentally, spiritually, sociably and sometimes physical by abuse, but I suggest that abuse and church hurt comes only by the hands of people in the church building or the religious organizations. It is the humans that are causing the turmoil and confusion not the theology of Christ, neither the concept nor relationship of God the Creator. We all must look past the hurt and misguidance from other believers, false leaders and the lack of knowledge of some pastors; all humans are flawed; we all make mistakes. The problem comes when we make people idol gods and begin to praise and worship them instead of God, and when they let us down, it tends to cause hurt and dissension. There is a passage in the Holy Writ (the Bible) that warns us of this: Matthew the 23rd chapter verse 12: Woe unto you, scribes and Pharisees (self-righteous people) which are insecure, for you close up to the kingdom of have against people; for even you yourself never go in and you do not allow others (the ones following your leadership) to cater in.

Time to recognize the people that are hindering you and I from our personal walk with God. We are realizing that no one is more important than our Creator God and our Savior, The Christ. No one should be able to cause us Believers to turn from our faith in

Christ and our personal encounters with God. We all must start looking past and beyond humans as a source of peace, deliverance and unconditional love and stay connected to God at all cost.

It is time to be of the faith that we do not have to blame God nor get angry with God about negative things that happen to us and our loved ones. When bad things happen, it is because of the human error and humans' sins. It is long past due that we all move on from just believing to a position of knowing in order to be able to stand strong in these evil days, having that peace, love, joy, and wisdom that surpasses all of our understandings. Yes, even the understandings from the Universe, you do know that God the Creator made the Universe and is over it too?

Jesus instructed doubting Thomas a disciple of his to not only have to see but believe. Because believing is the prerequisite of knowing that you know that you know, we have to experience faith in what we believe. But we cannot afford to stay stuck there because there may be someone or something that possibly could cause and convince you to doubt your faith in what you believe. I myself experienced this dilemma but thank God I was able to hold on to what I know; that God is real. Then I humbled myself, did even more research beyond what I had already researched. Beyond all the propaganda and convincing talk on YouTube and social media coming from intellectuals and so-called spiritual people of renown, and I held on to what I personally had encountered with who I know was the God of Love and Power! Now I am writing this book to make you aware of the possibility of you also considering denouncing our Lord and our God. Please beware and get grounded by knowing God The Creator. For the record, I choose to believe that Jesus is the Christ, my Savior, the Messiah. I do not need any more proof, because I do not rely on nor do I need a belief system to hold dear to that; I now Know!!!

So, is it then possible for me to have a relationship with God and follow Christ without the rituals in church settings…? I speak only for me. It obviously took being in a religious setting such as church for me to receive information in reference to understanding the works and instructions of Christ. It obviously took me being in church to develop my experience towards fellowshipping and agreeing with other believers in the faith. This definitely made me a Christian a follower of Jesus and His ways. So, do I after being in the church of Jesus The Christ since I was five years of age think I have to continue there in…? It all depends on what I am going for. I definitely do not have to be convinced that God is real because I, myself do not need to be involved in rituals to solidify who I am and who God is. So, I say this; I go for the camaraderie, the affinity support, friendship and mutual trust among people of like minds. Remember we all need one another. I also attend church to listen for confirmation of what I know, gain even more wisdom and have a collective opportunity to worship and praise God together with other believers in the faith.

Do I need to go to church for God to love and accept me? Of course not. Do I need to go to church to have or keep God relevant in my life? Most definitely not. Do I need to go to church in order to go to Heaven? No. Do I need to go to church to do right in the sight of God? No, again. But this is my personal stance, in my now or present state. Yes, there was a time when I had to go to church as much as possible. You have to make that decision on your own without being threatened, pushed hard or convinced by some through fear tactics or warnings of you being hell bound if you do not choose to go. However, if going to church helps you, please continue at least until you experience knowing God is real and God The Creator does love you unconditionally. Never go in bondage for anyone nor any religious affiliations. Going to church will never be the determining factor of your salvation, love or peace.

A real relationship with God, will when you fall in love with God, you will do better because you will grow to **reverence God and the works and person of** Christ outside of fear. So please get to know God as Creator of all. I pray you all to find a group of people to worship with at times, because oh how wonderful it is when children of the Most High God get together to fellowship. Just be aware and well advised that there are organizations, charismatic speakers, social media sights, along with so many other entities that are operating in the age of Enlightenment or Wokeness, and this can definitely cause a lot of us to doubt our faith in God and a need for a Savior. Please do not allow it to happen to you and pull you away from what you know is right for you.

12

The Power of Knowing is Contagious

To know is to perceive, learn, and understand, to know is a divine choice that we believers make spiritually. The word "know", is stated over 1300 times in the Bible. Its clear God ordained us to really know God to the best of our human ability. From my experiences, To Know is a mindset, that can be contagious, knowing can actually be transferrable, transmittable, spreading from one person to another by direct or indirect collaboration. This means I can operate in the mindset and belief having faith in that acknowledged belief or beliefs because I truly, ultimately and sincerely know a thing or entity to be truth. When I convey my thoughts of whoever and whatever I know to others, they then are in a position to hear me, and receive what I shared as fact and truth to the point of them then not only believing but agreeing with me, in the thing that I know. When they listen to a person that knows, and then agree, they obviously are agreeing because they really know it to be so. This is why the enemy tries hard to keep us all opposing one another, disagreeing with one another, and dividing us. Because the forces of evil know when believers actually agree in knowing, that's unity and that's power!

Scripture confirms my stance, lets read Matthew 18, verse 19. Jesus made a declaration with instruction, twice; he said "Again I say unto you, that if two of you shall agree on earth, as though both were touching, anything you ask it will be done for both of us of my father which is heaven. Verse 20 shares for where two or three are together in my name, I'm also there in the midst of them. Now let's go back up to verse 18 to make sure we are reading and understating in context. Jesus states: truly I say unto you, whatsoever you shall bind on earth or connect on earth shall be bound in heaven and whatsoever you shall do on earth shall be done or loosed in heaven. So, when we agree on what we know, we both shall experience evidence of what we agreed upon to happen or that we know will happen. Now that's the power of God and Gods true power is in love and knowing. So, if we want love, peace, assurance, victory, and power, we must operate in knowing.

    I respect everyone's views, but these are my views; I believe Jesus is Yeshua (was a real person). I choose not to operate in religious rituals, condemnation, and judgment from religious doctrine. I know God The Creator is real in my life. So I believe, understand and now come to know. I connect with God via spirit that's (mentally, psychologically, with soul, emotionally within my NUMA or conscience) what or who I choose to know is for my individual assurance. This helps me to never allow others to persuade me to believe and accept their ideologies by using error in scripture and misinterpretation even illustration or images to prove to me God is not real and Jesus or The Christ never existed. Because a book that brought slaves to America was called Jesus, the J and the name started 40 years prior and the fact that Jesus according to Revelation 1:14, nor Biblical characters were not European; all should realize that no human could live in the desert nations and remain European. And this is not an attempt to discredit my Caucasian brothers and sisters. This and human doctrines has and is misleading people, causing cognitive dissonance, the state of having inconsistent thoughts, beliefs, or attitudes, especially as relating behavioral decisions and attitude change. These constructive conversations are good because humans have an inquiring mind and are learned creatures with a brain, it's ok to obtain more knowledge, but it's not ok to even consider throwing away the Bible, your religious beliefs and your faith in God over new information.

Some Christians or Ex-Christians, Ex-Pastors or even ex-churchgoers and ex-religious believers of the faith in Jesus obviously are mentally operating in cognitive dissonance, solidifying that all beliefs systems are flawed and implies doubts. John 8:32; declares you shall know the truth and it will make you free. Knowing is power and sharing what you know can be contagious, and life-changing for those that hear you, listen and agree with you and because they agree that you are sincere about what you know, it can also manifest in their situations and life. There is power in agreement.

But we that know God is real, shouldn't be extreme or judgmental towards others that we want to believe and understand our truth. Our truth may not be absolute for others. We shouldn't be afraid of more knowledge, even when it discredits or debunks what we previously believed for years. Be open-minded yet use wisdom and your spiritual insight (Gods guidance) believers call this spiritual guidance; The Holy Spirit.

13

The Conclusion = A Revisiting of What I Know

How Do I Get to a Place of Knowing…?
Let's start here with the 8 "R" s; utilizing your brain in these areas.

The Conclusion = A Revisiting of What I Know

A. <u>Reflect</u> on your morals, your conscience, and your actions. These are attributes that molds and builds a person's character. But you have to be totally honest with yourself.

B. <u>Reconsider</u> all that's been taught and shared to you in reference to God, Religion and belief systems.

C. <u>Review & Research</u> the history of events leading towards the developments of the Bible, religious books, doctrines, and ritualism you've been privy to.

D. <u>Redirect</u> questions you've had that is never been answered thoroughly, also explanations given from someone else's intellect and understandings and direct those questions back to you, for you to analyze and ponder on.

E. <u>Revise</u> any past information that was found by you to be erroneous, misconceived, misleading and maybe even misinterpreted. How? You may ask… by following the R's in A through D and by extensive research.

F. <u>Remember</u> one event or happening that personally occurred in your life that no one can ever dispute nor discredit as being true and real in your life experiences. Hold on for dear life to that in which you know, that you have proof or evidence of as being your truth.

G. <u>Rethink</u> everything that was taught and shared with you, whether it was in a church setting and by leadership, also by any religious organizations or groups, even what you learned from the internet and social media. But as you do this, do it by consistently holding on to that which or what you know personally in reference to God.

After you have done these steps all starting with the Letter R, it is now time to become ok with thinking for yourself by allowing yourself to have peace within in order for you to make better decisions on what you choose to believe in conjunction with what or who you know in reference to God the Creator.

Let it be known every individual have their own truth, their own encounters with God, it is obviously personal in most cases, so do not ever second guest what you know as your personal encounter or experience with God. As Paul did in Philippians Chapter 3 as he warned us and told us believers to be aware of unbelievers, evil workers, and false circumcision. Paul shared with the believers of Christ, that we are the circumcision, which worship God in the Spirit and rejoice in Christ, and that we Believers should not have any confidence in our human or fleshly understanding. Paul and Apostle of Christ also stated that if he being circumcised on the eighth day of the stock of Israel of the Tribe of Benjamin in an Hebrew of the Hebrews who knew the law back and forth, one who persecuted the church, if anybody should think of having confidence in their flesh he probably should. But Paul counted all those accomplishments, his degree of knowledge and the loss of his connection for Christ, he counted all things but loss for the excellency of the knowledge of Jesus the Christ. Like many of us that are reading this book and have read Philippians chapter three, should do and that is to cease believing you know everything about all things because of your status, your title, your degree, and your connections and humble yourself and develop a desire to know God more than anything else. Especially to the point of you never stating you change your mind because you've been convinced that all of a sudden God is not real and that you also do not believe in the Christ.

    Be careful, so many are denouncing God and all that they professed to have believed. Why can't we all be of the mindset of Paul the Apostle of Christ, especially verse 10 of Philippians Chapter 3 when he declared loudly; Oh, that I may know God and the Resurrection Power God has. To fellowship with Christ sufferings, being made conformable unto his death. Again, and finally, the conclusion of the matter is that I Carter M. Head made a decision years ago to believe in Jesus The Christ and God. Though much consideration, research and going through the R's. I now can say with full honesty. I know God The Creator is real and I do choose to believe Yeshua (Jesus) is The Christ.

    I come to realize that you and I have to come to a mental and spiritual place of understanding that we have responsibility to not only allow God to connect with us on a personal level but we also have to work for, desire to and be consistent in seeking God for our self when we are mentally capable. We are definitely responsible for being awake or aware of propaganda, fake information and misinterpretation about the Bible. We must not allow what our personal experience entails about our encounter with God be disrupted to the point of any us denouncing the very God that we know is real.

Be careful of people out here in this world that are attempting to prove to you God is not real. These types of people are very articulate, charismatic and persuasive in their promulgating their information. Stand on what you know in reference to you knowing God is real in your life and if you choose to believe Jesus is the Messiah the Christ just know it is ok to believe whatever and in whoever you want. But be mindful to be able to stand with assurance on what you believe and that your believing did not only come by someone else teaching but by you obtained in knowledge and experiences. Then and only then will your faith in what you believe not be shaken, discredited or disannulled. Listen we will never know it all on this earth in reference to religion and God, but we surely can stand on that which we have come to know. Just learn to be ok with new truth or more truth, though it may be uncharted territory for you. Just seek knowledge about any unknown truth that directed to you as an individual. Remember truth comes with evidence, confirmation, agreement, love, power, peace, and assurance. I pray this book has helped you on your quest not only to get to know what you, believe but this book should also prompt you to eventually know that the Creator is Real and that you may have peace within knowing that.

After reading this book; you will realize, that you can have peace in saying and expressing to others that you can and have the right to think differently about your prior stance in your traditional religious beliefs. We must come to understand that we have to be careful with just going to church without using our brains. It's ok to bring your intellect and questions to church, because passivity can persuade us into error, unknowingly, to the point of possibly denouncing the very faith in the beliefs we once held dear to. We must be consistent in our convictions and morals by staying awake and conscious of who and what we know to be our truth, because obviously many of our morals, beliefs, and convictions we once stood fast on are being shattered right before our eyes and our lack of knowledge.

    First, don't allow anyone to disrespect your right to honor your truth and what you know, by convincing you that you're wrong. If you've come to know a thing after evaluating, seeking understanding, doing your research and being living proof by your life experience, no one will be able to get you to denounce God as Creator. Secondly, stay away from any organization or group that promotes and teach hatred, racism, divisions, and demise of any other human that's not being destructive towards others. Distance yourself from organizations that preach elitism because they advocate dominating elements in society. Their attitude and behavior regard themselves as belonging to a select group of people because of ancestry, intrinsic quality, high intellect, wealth, special skills, or experience, therefore thinking they deserve authority greater than that of others, this can be labeled discrimination, thinking you are better than others.

God loves us all equally and unconditionally; your titles, degrees, and accomplishments do not put any of us in a better place in God than others. We must humble ourselves, especially in leadership roles. Just know you as an individual is just as important and just as important and just as special as any other human on this planet because God designed you as such. Some people motive is to get us to put our hope in them and their abilities and resources. But when we begin to operate in the mindset of knowing God, we at that point will not have to depend on having hope in no other human in church or outside of the church. Our hope should be in God as Creator and unconditional love; this hope will ignite our enthusiasm to continue on a quest to really know God on a more personal level. Remember we humans have to believe in, hope for and have faith in something because it's actually therapeutic to our psyche. So, this book is not denouncing faith, belief, nor hope. This book is only saying use each of those in an effort to eventually knowing God to the point of not ever being persuaded that God is not real.

Thank you for reconsidering what you've been taught and choosing to move on forward in really knowing God without a shadow of a doubt. I'm happy for your efforts. Always reflect; this world would definitely be a better place for all humans to reside in each of us would consider seeking God in truth and love to the level of really knowing just a little about the true essence of God in each of our lives.

14

God or Extraterrestrial the Next Religious Dilemma

This chapter is restricted or limited to some believers and some non-believers. I choose to share some of my thoughts and beliefs on Unidentified Flying Craft, an object observed in the sky that is not readily identified as of Earthly origin because of its abilities to fly extremely faster than all known air craft and can maneuver beyond the technology of our space industries development. Also, the possibility of Extraterrestrials or Aliens, which are words describing human like, intelligent beings from other galaxies and planets, inside, and outside of our solar system. If you've read this book from the beginning up to this point, I'm sure you will not shut your mind down now, at the remote possibility of these entities being real today, and even if you choose not to believe, at least consider the possibility and do a little research. But before you discredit me and these writings, allow me to give you the reasonings that prompted me to elaborate on these subject matters.

I'm proposing the acknowledgement of a possible, unfiltered state of confusion and negative indictments coming against Religion as we've believed for centuries. Because if and when its revealed that Aliens exist, many will try to discredit Religion, and religious beliefs as a mindset, system, construct and a faith walk that's flawed, and not valid in reference to the God that's been worshipped. Many will try to tear down everything faith, and Religion presents and has taught us all. Many will ask questions of our faith and religious leaders that most will not be able to answer because of their lack of knowledge in this area and their failure to at least had looked into the possibility of Alien existence. Most preachers I know called Aliens demons or falling Angels. Our lack of understanding in reference to Extraterrestrials will cause chaotic circumstances in our belief system and in many cases the belief in The Christ and God. I believe many believers will denounce Jesus and the God of the Bible because of misguided facts about Aliens, their spacecraft, and their origins. I believe there would be a worldwide panic because of billions of people's ideologies and belief would be shattered. Too many questions would be unanswered, and millions will indeed turn from the teachings they once believed dearly in, millions will even denounce the very God that created them, blessed them, and proved to them unconditional love is real on a personal realization. Yet because so many only had faith in what they was taught to believe and never purposed in their hearts to really know

God The Creator and Savior to the point of nothing, no event and no one ever being able to convince or influence them that God can't be real and Jesus (Yeshua) could not have existed.

    This is why I wrote this book with the hopes of prompting people everywhere to really get serious on our quest to know God on a more personal level, beyond our beliefs and faith system. This doesn't mean to reject and turn from church or your religious belief. A lot of you need to increase your faithfulness, obedience, and consistence in your faith and fellowship. I do know millions of believers need to study, research, and seek God more fervently. Please never close your mind to information. Be always open to think, evaluate, research, and accept change even when it threatens what you and I have been taught for years.

Remember we evolve, things change, information is here to solidify or discredit. Just be rooted and grounded in what you believe by faith with knowing that you know, that you really know, God The Most High Creator is real in your life. Because I now know God is real, if there are Aliens out there, I don't have to rethink nor denounce my belief in what I know to be truth and that is: Creator God Yahweh as according to my beliefs. In which I acknowledge humans are incapable of actually pronouncing the Creator's name. But we give God names in order to relate with one another and that's ok. Most of us understand God can't be described thoroughly by human intellect or brain capacity. But that I do now know is good enough for me to stand on for eternity and beyond, no matter how anyone subscribes God as being. Some say the Universe is their guide, but God created the Universe, some will say that Aliens established their human existence on earth, but God created Aliens. So, there's nothing that's in existence that God the Creator didn't create. God is above all. I thank God for gracing me to write this book, one of the most difficult but rewarding projects I've ever had the privilege of doing thus far in my life and this work has really advanced and solidified my open-mindedness, intuitions, consciousness, intellect, and heart for the truth (my gut feeling), along with my extensive research. I now know with my entire heart mind and soul that God is Real and Alive.

15

For My Christian Pastors and Leadership

I, Carter, a servant of the Most High God humbly beseech you, ministers and preachers of the Gospel of the Kingdom of God and Jesus The Christ (Act 8:12), to please adhere to with an open mind and humility of soul, along with a desire for God's people to be feed the meat of the word, in order for each of them to grow and be able to stand against the wiles and trickery of Satan devices. We really should revisit Hebrews chapter 7 verses 1 through 6 in which the writer instructs and mandates us preachers to move forward from only just teaching milk and began a series of teaching strong meat. Let's move on from what I call Elementary teachings unless its only for new believers.

Too many are leaving the church, Jesus, and eventually denouncing the very God that brought them out and blessed them, maybe because the milk has spoiled, and they desire meat because they are wrestling as adults with more. Hebrews 5:12-14 sums it up and precedes Hebrews 6: 1-3. Quote "For when for the time you ought to be Teachers, you have need that one teach you again which be the first principles of the oracles or word of God; and are become such as have need of milk, and not of strong meat for everyone that useth milk is unskillful or not acquainted in the word of righteousness: for he is a baby. But strong meat belongth to them that are of full age, even those who by reason of use have their sense trained to discern both good and evil <u>Therefore</u>, leaving the principles of the teaching of Christ, let us go on unto maturity, etc."

    It's not saying don't teach and preach the doctrine of Christ. Its saying don't allow the same old same old continuance to be a hindrance towards people moving on forwards with more and new knowledge. Be mindful of your generational traditions. I'm not speaking against anyone's traditions, I'm only saying don't allow cultural traditions to stop or prevent the strong meat of God's word to be ministered allowing with new ideas, new information and opened minded (broader) ways of thinking. Be reminded people of God, none of us theologians, scholars, ministers, none believers nor preacher, Know everything there is to know in reference to Jesus The Christ because in 33 years on earth he did much more than we ever read about from the Bible and other historical writing. John 21:25 shares to us that the whole world couldn't hold the books that would be written of all the things Jesus did. We only know a small portion. Stay humble, knowing this. There's so much more to learn; please stay open minded and awake.

We must do more.

We must reevaluate what we are doing.

We must be open for changing of the times.

We must operate in more unity towards a greater, loving, empathetic and compassionate work in God our Creator for the soul purpose of servanthood and advancement in the Kingdom of God.

Thank you, Family of God.

May Peace and Blessing always be upon you.

About the Author

Carter M. Head is a life coach, a minister, and is one of the most dynamic, realistic, and sought-out conference speakers. Carter is a graduate of Andersonville Theological Seminary and Alumni of West Georgia College. Carter founded and established many outreach organizations in reference to feeding and clothing the indigent. Carter also established the YL2 (Youth Leadership League of Henry County, GA), and he coproduced three live stage plays emphasizing on the issues of our youth. Carter established the mentoring group called B.I.N.O. In addition, Carter is an author, grant writer, marriage counselor, and philanthropist.

Other Books by the Author

- ◊ Lying Mirrors
- ◊ Unity for What?
- ◊ Questions with No Answers
- ◊ Am I Trump?

Direct all inquiries and correspondence to:

Heads Up Publications
c/o Carter M. Head
P.O Box 162593
Atlanta, GA 30321

www.ingramcontent.com/pod-product-compliance
Lightning Source LLC
Chambersburg PA
CBHW070610010526
44118CB00012B/1481